AUSTRIA

Travel Guide Book

A Comprehensive 5-Day Travel Guide to Vienna,
Austria & Unforgettable Austrian Travel

• *Travel Guides to Europe Series* •

Passport to European Travel Guides

Eye on Life Publications

Vienna, Austria Travel Guide Book
Copyright © 2016 Passport to European Travel Guides

ISBN 10: 1519132956
ISBN 13: 978-1519132956

~

Other Travel Guide Books by Passport to European Travel Guides

Top 10 Travel Guide to Italy

Florence, Italy

Rome, Italy

Venice, Italy

Naples & the Amalfi Coast, Italy

Paris, France

Provence & the French Riviera, France

Top 10 Travel Guide to France

London, England

Barcelona, Spain

Amsterdam, Netherlands

Santorini, Greece

Greece & the Greek Islands

Berlin, Germany

Munich, Germany

Istanbul, Turkey

Budapest, Hungary

Prague, Czech Republic

Brussels, Belgium

"Vienna is the gate to Eastern Europe."
—*Niki Lauda*

Table of Contents

• Map of Vienna, Austria •

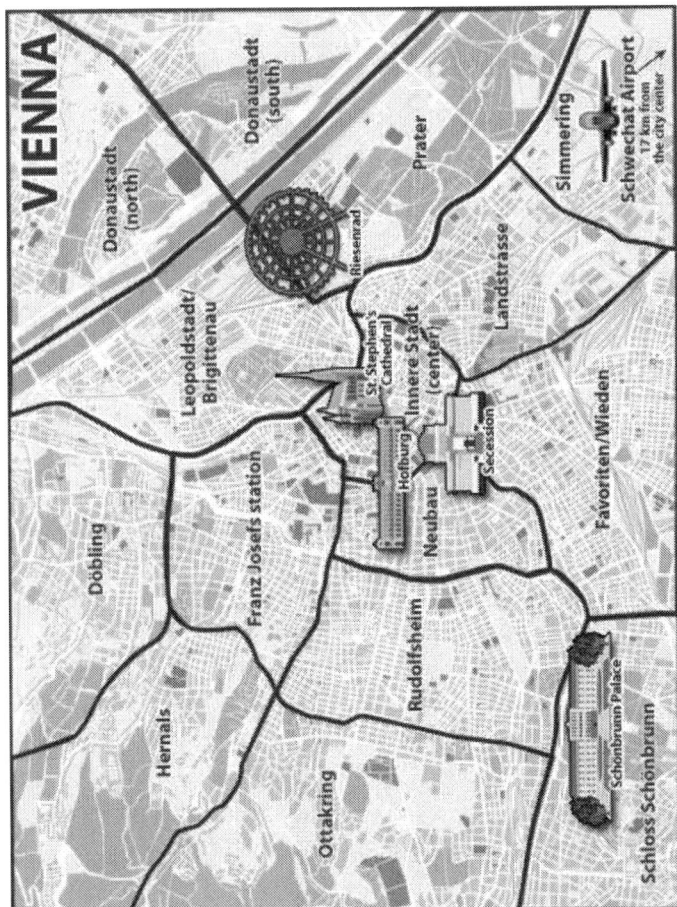

© Image Courtesy: www.viennahotels.it

• Introduction •

Vienna, Austria. "The City of Dreams." A smoothly blended mixture of Gothic cathedrals and trendy dance music festivals, **Vienna** (Wien in German) is the European city that certainly feeds the appetite for **high culture**. The live street performances, the famous art galleries and fine dining experiences will have you wanting to return for multiple visits — guaranteed!

In this 5-day guide to Vienna, you'll find a variety of our top recommendations and helpful tips to prepare you for having the best travel experience in this fairytale of a locale! **Read over the insider tips** carefully and familiarize yourself with the information on preparing for your trip. **Every traveler** has different preferences, and we've included a wide range of recommendations to suit all tastes and budgets.

You're welcome to follow our detailed **5-day itinerary** to the letter, or you can **mix and match** the activities at your own discretion.

Most importantly, we know you're sure to have a great time and enjoy the magical city that is Vienna!

Enjoy!

• City Snapshot •

Language: German

Local Airports: Vienna International Airport (VIE)

Currency: Euro | € (EUR)

Country Code: 43

Emergencies: Dial 112 (for all emergencies) 133 (police) 122 (fire) 144 (ambulance)

• Before You Go... •

✓ Have a Passport

If you don't already have one, you'll need to apply for a passport in your home country a good two months before you intend to travel, to avoid cutting it too close. **You'll need to find a local passport agency**, complete an application, take fresh photos of yourself, have at least one form of ID and pay an application fee. **If you're in a hurry**, you can usually expedite the application for a 2-3 week turnaround at an additional cost.

✓ Need a Visa?

The US State Department provides a wealth of country-specific information for American travelers, including **travel alerts and warnings**, the location of the **US embassy in each country**, and of course, **whether or not you need a visa** to travel there!
http://travel.state.gov/content/passports/english/country.html

Vienna adheres to Austrian visa requirements for entry. U.S. citizens do not need a visa for stays less than 3 months and the passport must be valid for at least 6 months after the date of arrival.

✓ Healthcare

Prior to your trip, you should **purchase a travel insurance** to cover any medical expenses in case you should become ill or have an accident while in Austria. **If you have general health insurance**, you should first check with them to see what coverage you have (if any) when traveling abroad. This is always the best way to go, since whether or not you have your own insurance can greatly impact the type of care you receive, the when, where and how.

Visitors from within Europe need to carry a valid EHIC (European Health Insurance Card) and present it at the time of treatment.

✓ Set the Date

The mild, continental seasons of spring and fall are the perfect times to visit Vienna if you want to avoid big crowds. The months of **June, July and August** are **peak months** when the Viennese sun attracts hoards of travelers.

Of course, the ideal time for skiing is during the winter months of **December and January**, but the temperatures plummet. However frigid it might get, you'll find everyone is still in a jolly festive spirit at this time of year!

✓ Pack

• We recommend **packing only the essentials** needed for the season in which you'll be traveling. By far, the most important thing to pack is a good pair of **walking shoes** (water-resistant if you're traveling in colder months, and comfortable, light sandals or sneakers to walk good distances in warmer months).

• If you're planning on visiting the beautiful **cathedrals of Vienna**, be sure to pack **clothes that appropriately cover** your shoulders and legs. **In the colder months,** bring a warm sweater, clothes you can layer, and a rain jacket or umbrella. And always pack **sunscreen, sunglasses, and a hat.**

• **A backpack** can be handy during the day when you go out sightseeing and collecting souvenirs, particularly when getting on and off buses, boats, trains or trams.

• If you don't speak German, be sure to pack a good **conversational German phrase guide** to bring along with you. You'll find people a lot friendlier toward you if you don't go around assuming they speak your language.

• **Hand sanitizer** is always great to have along with you when traveling.

• **Medication.** Don't forget to have enough for the duration of your trip. It's also helpful to have a **note from your physician** in case you're questioned for carrying a certain quantity.

• A simple **first aid kit** is always a good idea to have in your luggage, just in case.

• You can bring one or two **reusable shopping bags** for bringing souvenirs home.

• **Travelers from outside Europe** will need to bring along a **universal electrical plug converter** that can work for both lower and higher voltages. This way you'll be able to plug in your cell phones, tablets, curling irons, etc., during the trip.

• Be sure to **leave expensive jewels and high-priced electronics at home**. Like most major cities and tourist attractions, thieves and pickpockets abound. Avoid making yourself a target.

• **Take pictures of your travel documents and your passport** and email them to yourself before your trip. This can help in the unfortunate event they are lost or stolen.

• **Pack well,** but be sure to leave room for souvenirs!

✓ Phone Home

How will you call home from Austria? Does your cell phone company offer service while abroad? **What are their rates?**

There are many ways to **call home** from Europe that are inexpensive or completely free.

You may also **sign up for roaming or Internet hotspot** through your own cell phone provider. You can also use Skype, WhatsApp, Viber, or many other voice-over IP providers that are entirely free.

You can also buy a cheap, **pre-paid local phone or phone chip** for your phone—which also gives you a local phone number. **Calling cards** are used less and less these days, but they're also an option.

✓ Currency Exchange

Vienna uses the **euro** (€) as its currency (same as most of Western and Central Europe). Check out the **currency exchange** rates prior to your trip. You can do so using the following or many other online currency exchange calculators, or through your bank. **For the best rates**, we recommend **waiting until you arrive in Vienna** to buy euros, but be mindful of high commission rates in the airport.
http://www.xe.com/currencyconverter

Use ATMs for the **best exchange rates**, they're everywhere; buying euros at the airport, at your hotel or in a store will almost always cost more.

Also, make sure your bank knows you'll be traveling abroad. This way you avoid having foreign country transactions flagged and declined, which can be extremely inconvenient!

✓ Contact Your Embassy

In the unfortunate event that you should lose your passport or be victimized while away, **your country's embassy** will be able to help you. Be sure to give your itinerary and contact information to a close **friend or family member**, then also contact your embassy with your emergency contact information before you leave.

✓ Your Mail

Ask a neighbor to **check your mailbox** while you're away or visit your local post office and request a hold.

Overflowing mailboxes are a dead giveaway that no one's home.

• Getting in the Mood •

Here are a few great books and films set in or about **Vienna** that we recommend you watch in preparation for your trip to this magical locale!

What to Read:

A definite must-read for the prospective Viennese traveler is: **Waiting for Sunrise** by William Boyd. An acclaimed psychological thriller set in Vienna at the dawn of the 20th century, this page-turning story about a young British actor who travels to Vienna in hopes of curing an embarrassing problem is one of our favorites!

And for a true journey of superb imagination, don't miss **The Little Book** by Selden Edwards. Vienna comes alive with Wheeler Burden once he leaves his native San Francisco 1988 and finds himself in 1897 Vienna! Everyone from Sigmund Freud to Mark Twain crosses Wheeler's path. It's a stunning debut novel!

What to Watch:

There are many films that can get you completely besotted with the city of Vienna, but no more so than two of our favorites below:

The Third Man is a timeless classic that earned an Oscar in 1949 and stars the legendary Orson Welles.

Considered one of the greatest films of all time, it was filmed on location and provides an interesting experience of the city. If you enjoy the movie, you might like to take The Third Man **walking tour** dedicated to the iconic movie. Highly recommended!

For info about the tour:
http://www.wien.info/en/sightseeing/tours-guides/third-man

And the enduring film **Amadeus** gives fascinating insight into the traumatic life of the classical composer, Mozart and the jealous composer who is said to have shortened Mozart's life. The musical legacy of the city truly shines in this eight-time Academy Award winning masterpiece.

• Local Tourist Information •

Vienna is a very tourist-friendly city and visitors are certainly well looked after. There are tourism offices scattered all over the city and they can make your sightseeing that much more pleasurable.

The main website is: http://www.wien.info/en

Tourist Info Main Station
Address: Am Hauptbahnhof 1, 1100, Vienna
Phone Number: +43-1-24555
Open from 9:00am - 5:00pm Monday to Sunday

Tourist Information Vienna Airport
Located in the Arrival Hall
Open daily from 7:00am - 10:00pm

Tourism Vienna
Address: Albertinaplatz/Maysedergasse
Phone Number: +43-1-24555
Open daily 9:00am - 7:00pm

Wiener Linien Tram and Bus Lines
Location: Hauptbahnhof U1
6:30 am - 6:30 pm

• About the Airports •

Located about 11 miles outside central Vienna, the **Vienna International Airport** consists of four terminals and is the main airport servicing visitors from all over the world. For flight schedules and more, visit the airport website at:
http://www.viennaairport.com/en

• How Long is the Flight? •

• **The flight to Vienna** from **New York City** is approx. 9 hours

• **From Chicago:** approx. 9.5 hours

• **From Los Angeles:** approx. 14 hours

• **From Toronto:** approx. 8.5 hours

• **From Moscow:** approx. 2 hours 45 min

• **From London:** approx. 2 hours 15 min

• **From Paris:** approx. 2 hours

• **From Hong Kong:** approx. 14 hours 40 min

• **From Cape Town:** approx. 14 hours 30 min

• **From Sydney:** approx. 24 hours

• Overview of Vienna •

The capital city of Austria, Vienna is one of the largest cities by population in the European Union. Bordering Germany, the city has adopted the language as well as many German traditions, although with a particular Viennese flavor.

The home of the world's first psychoanalyst, Sigmund Freud, Vienna was nicknamed "The City of Dreams" as well as the "The City of Music."

While some might argue that the **flavor of Vienna** is captured in the **rich coffee** of the café-driven lifestyle the locals embrace, we think the culture also flourishes in so many of the experiences that await its many tourists.

Towering cathedrals grace the skyline of the city, reminding inhabitants of the Roman and Celtic influences of medieval times.

Home to legends of **baroque music**, no other city has welcomed and nurtured the musical pedigree of greats such as **Mozart, Beethoven, Haydn, and Brahms**, just to name a few of the legends who worked and studied here.

Vienna is also rich in theater, buzzing on a theatrical high throughout the year — only the costumes change.

Without a doubt, Vienna is the picture-perfect, culture-rich destination everyone can enjoy!

• Insider Tips For Tourists •

Etiquette

• **Proper etiquette in Vienna** is largely based on one's class and upbringing. Visitors and tourists tend to be regarded with patience and lenience.

• **Nudity in public is commonplace** in designated areas of Vienna. To identify if public nudity is permitted at certain pools, lakes or beaches, look for **'FKK'** signage.

• **Punctuality** is very important in Austria.

Time Zone

Vienna is in the Central European Time Zone (UTC+1:00). There is a **6-hour time difference** between New York and Vienna (Vienna is ahead on the clock). When it's 8 AM in New York, it's 2 PM in Vienna.

The format for abbreviating dates in Europe is different from the US. They use: **day/month/year**. So for example, August 23, 2025 is written in Europe as 23 August 2025, or 23/8/25.

Saving Time & Money

• Buying a **Vienna Pass** is one of the first things you can do to save time and money, particularly when it comes to hopping on and off the tram or train system that services Vienna. The card not only provides **unlimited travel around the city**, but most of the city's **main attractions** accept the pass for discounts on food, drink and special events. Visit:
http://www.viennapass.com

• Be sure to get yourself a **map of the routes** that are serviced by the public transport systems and have it on hand to check what the major stops are and which are connected by trams, trains and bus lines. These are available in the airport and train stations or from tourist information desks.

• Take advantage of the **complimentary breakfast** at your hotel and **eat well** so you start the morning with enough energy to fuel a long day of sightseeing.

• **Lipizzaner performances** are heavy on the pocket and very popular so need to be booked well in advance, but you can catch the training sessions at a **fraction of the cost** in the middle of the day without reserving a seat. **The Spanish Riding School** practices Tuesday to Saturday in the Hapsburg Winter Palace from 10 am - noon.
http://www.srs.at/en_US/start-en

Tipping

In restaurants, tips are generally included in your final bill but it is common courtesy to round up to the nearest whole euro. **For example,** €17,38 is rounded up to €18. If you use a credit card, any tip is expected in cash.

In taxis, tipping is expected in a similar fashion, round up to the nearest euro.

In hotels, tipping is not required but a couple euros can be given to the bellman and cleaning staff in appreciation for their efforts.

When You Have to Go

Marked with 'WC' signage, public bathrooms are readily available in and around Vienna, especially near the popular tourist sites. There are also public bathrooms available in the local transport terminals, like the bus and train stations.

Most public restrooms require you to pay around €0,50 for use and most are not open before 9 am or after 6 pm, except in the train stations where they are open 24 hours.

Taxes

The Value Added Tax (or VAT) is a consumption tax. The standard rate in Austria is about 20%. Reduced VAT rates apply for pharmaceuticals, passenger transport, admission to cultural and entertainment events, hotels, restaurants (10%) and on foodstuffs, medical and books (4%). The Austrian VAT is part of the European Union's value added tax system.

Visitors from outside Europe may be eligible for a **VAT refund** if certain criteria are met: 1) you do not live in Europe 2) you must be leaving within 3 months of the purchase 3) purchase must be made in a shop or business that participates in the Retail Export Scheme or Tax Free Shopping program 4) purchases must meet the minimum of about €75 spent in one shop at one time.

The process to claim the reimbursement is quite laborious and involves applying to either the **Global Refund Organization or Austria Refund**. This can be done on site in the shop where you have made your purchase — the shop assistant needs to complete the form and the bill must be enclosed in the refund envelope, which you will need to submit to the customs office when you leave the country.

Alternatively, once back in your home country you may mail the documentation to one of the organization's offices.

Phone Calls

The international dialing code for Austria is +43 for those calling you. When dialing out, preface the number with 00 and then the code of the country + the area code and number you want to call:

- U.S and Canada: 1

- U.K.: 44

- China: 86

- Australia: 61

Electricity

Electricity in Europe uses **220-240 volts** alternating at 50 cycles per second (by comparison, the U.S. uses 110 volts, alternating at 60 cycles per second.) Not only are the voltages and frequencies **different in Europe**, but the socket plugs are as well. **So we must stress** that travelers from outside of Europe need to bring along a **power and plug converter** to ensure that your phones, tablets, hairdryers, curling irons, laptops, etc., will work while you're abroad—and also won't be fried by the higher voltage they weren't built to handle.

Some hotels will provide these in their rooms, however they are readily available for purchase at most airport shopping facilities.

In Emergencies

The catchall number for emergencies throughout the European Union is **112** but for specific services: **dial 133 for police, 122 for the fire brigade, and 144 for an ambulance**.

German Phrases For Emergencies:

I need help, please!	Ich brauch hilfe bitte!
Please send the police/ambulance/fire brigade	Bitte senden Sie die Polizei/krankenwagen/feuer wehr
I don't understand	Ich verstehe nicht

Pharmacies in Vienna are typically open Monday to Friday 8:00 am - 6:00 pm, and Saturdays mornings. Each pharmacy posts the location of the next closest open pharmacy.

For phone inquiries, call 01/1550 if you speak German or have someone with you who can.

Holidays

• New Year's Day: January 01
• Epiphany: January 06
• Easter Monday: April 06
• Labour Day: May 01
• Ascension Day: May 14
• Whit Monday: May 25

- Corpus Christi: June 04

- Assumption Day: August 15

- National Day of Austria: October 26

- All Saints' Day: November 01

- Immaculate Conception: December 08

- Christmas Day: December 25

Hours of Operation

The public transport system in Vienna runs daily from 5:00 am to midnight. Subway lines run 24 hours Fridays, Saturdays and the evenings before holidays. These trains are at 15-minute intervals.

Stores and shops typically open 9:00 am – 6:30 pm during the week, and until 5:00 or 6:00 on Saturdays. There are some **main shopping centers** that stay open until 8:00 or 9:00 pm weekdays.

In Vienna, lunch is typically 12:30 pm - 1:30 pm.

Gas stations are open 24 hours on all major highways.

Banks are typically open 8:00 am - 3:00 pm on weekdays, and until 5:30 pm on Thursdays. They are closed on weekends, but ATMs are readily available.

Museums are generally open 10:00 am to 5:00 pm. Some art galleries have one night a week where they stay open until 9:00 pm.

Post Office hours are usually from 8:00 am - 6:00 pm weekdays and closed on weekends.

Money

As mentioned, the currency in Austria is the **euro** (€). Check out the currency exchange rates prior to your trip, online or through your bank. To obtain euros, we recommend waiting until you get to Vienna and using the local ATMs.

There are small exchange booths about the city where euros can be bought, but the commission fees are higher than at a bank.

Paying by preloaded travel card is an option as well as using your credit card, but be aware that fees will be levied for purchases outside of the country of origin.

Some places in Vienna may accept U.S. dollars, but not many, and the exchange rate will usually be higher.

We also recommend simply **using your credit cards** for good exchange rates on purchases, but watch for **unnecessary fees.** When using your credit cards, always choose to **pay in euros** vs. dollars if you're given the option. Paying in dollars will usually cost you more in fees.

Almost no one uses **traveler's checks** anymore, so we don't recommend them. There are many easier and safer ways to handle money while traveling. Unless it cannot be avoided, **never carry more than €200 on you at a time,** in case of theft. It's easy to simply withdraw cash from the many ATMs in Vienna or use your credit cards.

Climate and Best Times to Travel

The best time to visit Vienna really depends on your personal preferences and your budget, but we recommend spring and fall. The **continental climate** means the **summers are hot and humid,** but temperamental and can change without warning. **July and August** are peak travel months in Vienna and prices all around reflect that fact. Many hotels are full and the main attractions increase their ticket prices as well.

If you are looking for a **traditionally snowy Christmas, December or January** is when you should plan to visit Vienna. But come prepared with the right attire!

Transportation

As mentioned before, the public transport system in Vienna is efficient and safe. The S-Bahn and the U-Bahn systems make up the bus, tram and train services that cover the city.

Children under 6 travel free in Vienna and kids under 15 travel free on public holidays, Sundays and on school holidays.

Tickets are available for purchase in the metro stations and they must be validated before you board. There are **blue machines** at the entrance of the underground stations that **must stamp the ticket**, unless it was purchased directly from the tram or bus driver.

Different passes are available for extended use and these include an 8-day pass, a student pass and a strip of 4 tickets, which are all available from ticket offices and some tobacconists shops.

Driving

As we mentioned, Vienna has an excellent public transportation system so we don't recommend driving unless you're familiar with the area and have driven there before. Renting cars can be expensive and parking can be pricey and hard to find in many areas.

However, if you do end up driving, please be sure you study the **traffic regulations** and print out your driving routes; or ensure your rental car has an English-language GPS you know how to use before you enter the Austrian roadways.

Take care if you do decide to drive in Vienna, as it is an old city and some of the roads are not wide enough to accommodate two vehicles at a time.

You should also note that trams and bicycles take priority over cars on the roads in Vienna. **Pedestrians** have the right of way at all times and you are required to stop at the crossings to allow for those on foot to cross.

• Tours •

Vienna By Bike

Pedal Power offers a variety of tours in and around Vienna where travelers can see monasteries, national parks or just enjoy the natural beauty of the region at a leisurely pace. It's one of our favorites!

Location Info:

Pedal Power
Address: Ausstellungsstraße 3
Phone Number: +43 1 729 72 34
Website:
http://www.pedalpower.at/z_english/Trips/daybiketrips.php

Bike Experience Vienna is a tour company that takes adventure seekers off the beaten track into the countryside of Vienna giving tourists a view of the woods and wine farms and it begins with a 15 minute pedal to the outskirts of the city. Lots of fun!

Location Info:

Bike Experience Vienna
Address: Billrothstrasse 45/4/10
Phone Number: +43 699 12628212
Website: http://www.bike-experience.at/en

Vienna By Boat

DDSG Blue Danube is great for a culinary and musical experience on the waters of the world-famous Danube River! The 6-boat operation offers a variety of tours from the lazy tugboat style cruisers to the catamarans that will get you down the river to Bratislava in record time.

Location Info:

DDSG Blue Danube
Address: Handelskai 265
Phone Number: +43 1 58 880 0
Website: http://www.ddsg-blue-danube.at/eng/index

National Park Boat takes visitors into the National Park of Donau-Auen to enjoy the untouched natural landscape or "jungle" of Vienna, The Lobau. This tour lasts about 4.5 hours and currently runs between May and October.

Location Info:

National Park Boat
Address: Salztorbrücke, departs from Franz-Josefs Quay
Phone Number: +43 1 4000 49495
Website:
http://www.wien.info/en/sightseeing/green-vienna/lobau-jungle

Vienna By Bus

Vienna Sightseeing offers a Hop On Hop Off Tour, giving tourists the luxury of choosing the sites they want to visit and planning an itinerary that suits their interests. We think it's one of the best ways to experience the city, especially for families and groups.

Location Info:

Vienna Sightseeing — Hop On Hop Off
Address: Opernpassage, Top 3,
Phone Number: +43 1 712 46 83 0
Website:
https://www.viennasightseeing.at/en/hop-on-hop-off

Cityrama provides a widespread road adventure that includes everything from following in the footsteps of Mozart, to stopping to ride a giant Ferris wheel! One of the more popular tours is seeing Vienna by night, an offering that runs in the spring and summer months.

Location Info:

Cityrama
Address: Opernpassage, Top 3
Phone Number: +43 1 504 75 00
Website: http://www.cityrama.at

Vienna By Minibus or Car

For a tour of the cities highlights in the comfort of a minivan, **Viator** has great options for 3-hour, 5-hour and 7-hour tours that take you to the city's best cultural and historical hotspots.

Location Info:

Viator
Phone Number: +888-651-9785
Website:
http://www.viator.com/tours/Vienna/Private-Tour-Vienna-City-Highlights-Tour/d454-3943VIENNA_P

A private tour with a dedicated guide is the best way to see the city if you don't have time on your side. We highly recommend **Wienguide Private Tours.** Peter Scheiber is a state approved tour guide who gets you around the city, and even into the woods if you want!

Location Info:

Wienguide Tours
Address: Gassergasse 41/4/10
Phone Number: +43 660 446 6045
Website: http://www.wienguide.net/vienna-guide-english

Try Special Interest or Walking Tours

Foodies will love the variety of **culinary tours** on offer in Vienna! Tour the city's great restaurants, taverns, coffee shops and more!

Location Info:

Culinary Tours of Vienna
Website: http://www.wien.info/en/shopping-wining-dining/culinary-tours

Explore the city of Vienna in a **cozy horse-drawn carriage** with the **Viennese fiakers**. Choose between a short approximately 20-minute ride, or the longer approx. 40-minute ride and enjoy!

Location Info:

Fiaker Carriage Ride Through Vienna
Phone Number: +43 699 181 540 22

Website:
http://www.wien.info/en/sightseeing/fiaker-horse-drawn-carriage

Enjoy Mozart? You'll love the divine **Vienna Mozart Evening!** This specialty tour includes a scrumptious gourmet dinner and concert at Vienna's celebrated Musikverein concert hall.

Location Info:

Vienna Mozart Evening
Phone Number: +888-651-9785
Website:
http://www.viator.com/tours/Vienna/Vienna-Mozart-Evening-Gourmet-Dinner-and-Concert-at-the-Musikverein/d454-2322PASS

The Viator has a great walking tour of the city through the eyes of locals! **The Vienna City Walking Tour** lasts about 2.5 hours and an experienced guide covers all the city highlights, including St. Stephen's Cathedral, Hofburg Imperial Palace and the Spanish Riding School.

Location Info:

Vienna City Walking Tour
Phone Number: +888-651-9785
Website:
http://www.viator.com/tours/Vienna/Vienna-City-Walking-Tour/d454-3943WALK

Original Vienna Tours is a company that appeals to the alternative traveler looking for something out of the ordinary. They offer pub-crawls and music tours for those looking for an 'on the ground' experience. The tours feature graffiti art, community projects and Vienna's modern pop culture spots. Highly recommended!

Location Info:

Original Vienna Tours
Address: Mariahilfer Gürtel 21
Phone Number: +43 664 585 6206
Website: http://free-vienna-tours.com/tours

The Sigmund Freud Tour features the life and work of—you guessed it—Sigmund Freud, the world's chief psychoanalyst! This walking tour guides you through the sites associated with his groundbreaking works. An accredited guide leads the approximately 2-hour tour, which concludes at Vienna's fabulous Sigmund Freud Museum.

Location Info:

Sigmund Freud Tour Vienna
Address: Stättermayergasse 6
Website:
http://www.sigmundfreudtourvienna.com

• 5 Days in Vienna! •

Enjoy this 5-day itinerary for a well-balanced and easy-going experience! Modify or adjust if you like! Also, be sure to **check websites or call ahead** for the most recent hours and pricing information. Enjoy!

• Day 1 •

Once you arrive at your hotel (or wherever you're staying) relax a bit, get settled and then freshen up before venturing out to begin your Viennese adventure. (It's best to arrive in the morning.)

Unless you'll be driven around, familiarizing yourself with the city and its transport system is always a great idea. Purchase yourself a Vienna Pass or travel pass at the metro stations and hop on the Ringstrasse line that will take you the entire way around the city by tram. You can find the station closest to your accommodation by using your **city map.**

The city center is a good place to begin your Viennese experience, with the iconic **St. Stephan's Cathedral,** right in the heart of Vienna. You can climb the towers and enjoy a view across Vienna like no other.

It may be time for some refreshment after the tower climb and there is no better place to experience the coffee/café culture of the city than at **Café Landtmann.** Here you find all the traditional Austrian cakes and pastries, which, combined with their espresso and milk (Wiener Melange), teeters on the edge of sheer decadence!

The **mumok** is Vienna's most prestigious 20th-century art gallery with over 9,000 artworks on display. The gallery needs a few hours of your time to really digest what it has to offer. From Picasso to Klee, the mumok museum always has exciting features happening! And there are even workshops to take part in.

On your way back to your hotel, if you're not too tired, stop by **Lutz** for a beer or cocktail, and maybe a bite to eat! Who knows? You may want to stay a while longer...the atmosphere is laid back and the prices are budget-friendly.

Location Information:

St. Stephan's Cathedral
Address: Stephansplatz 3
Phone Number: +43 1 513 76 48

Website: http://www.stephansdom.at

Café Landtmann
Address: Universitätsring 4
Phone Number: +43 124 100 100
Website: http://www.landtmann.at

mumok
Museum moderner Kunst
Stiftung Ludwig Wien
Address: Museumsplatz 1
Phone Number: +43 1 525 00 0
Website: https://www.mumok.at/en

Lutz
Address: Mariahilfer Str. 3
Phone Number: +43 1 585 3646
Website: http://www.lutz-bar.at

• Day 2 •

Start the day with a hearty (but not heavy) breakfast at your hotel, as the day is going to be an active one!

Now that you have a better grasp on the layout of the city, you can head off to one of the 110 rental stations that **Citybike Wien** offers and ride down the well-maintained paths alongside the Danube. On your way there, stop at a Billa supermarket and pick up a sandwhich or pastry for lunch.

On your way back, if your legs are up to it, there is the cycle path that follows the **Ringstrasse** around the inner city past the **buildings of parliament, the state opera house, and the theater. The imperial palace (Hofburg Palace)** is also along this route and it takes you right through the City Park where you can stop and take a breath at the **Johann Strauss Monument.**

There are seven major biking paths around Vienna and all are well marked. And if you're too tired to manage the return trip, you can always hop onto one of the trains. Bikes are allowed on local trains if there is enough space, although the entire route is 2,4 miles long (4,5 kilometers), which should not be a problem for most ameteur cyclists.

To plan your route, there are various tools at your disposal. The **biking map of Vienna** is particularly helpful as it gives distances and average times from one spot to the next, allowing you to plan your breaks more accurately and avoid getting back to the hotel in the dark. You may even choose the type of bike you want to use and the pace at which you pedal.

Biking maps are usually available free of charge at most Vienna hotels and tourist information sites.

At the end of your vigorous day, if you still have the energy, the vinotheques and wine bars offer a modern take on the traditional wine tasting experience. **Pub Klemo Wine Bar** has a layout that encourages you to sip the local 'Gemischter Satz' whilst recovering from the day's activities and enjoying some delicious Viennese cuisine.

Location Information:

Citybike Wien
E-mail Queries to: kontakt@citybikewien.at
Website: http://www.citybikewien.at

Pub Klemo Wine Bar
Address: Margaretenstraße 61, Vienna
Phone Number: +43 699 110 913 32
Website: http://www.pubklemo.at

• Day 3 •

After yesterday's rather busy stint on the bicycle, today you may appreciate a little less activity with a lot more culture!

The cuisine in Vienna is as rich as the city's musical and theatrical history. So instead of breakfast at your hotel, today we recommend checking out the most extensive **variety of egg dishes** on offer in Vienna. **Joma**, opens at 8:00 am and is the typical **street side café** but with a not-so-typical menu. You'll love the atmosphere here!

Next, nothing beats the grace and beauty of **dancing horses**, and the **Spanish Riding School** has practices in the morning from 10:00 am to noon at a fraction of the cost of night performances. Bookings can be made on the website for the formal performances or tickets for the practices can be bought on site.

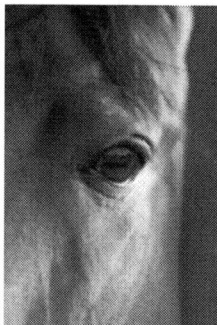

For lunch today, we recommend the bagel house hidden down the narrow alleyways of Ledererhof Street. **The Brezl Gwolb** caters to seekers of traditional Austrian dishes—that is if you can find a seat amongst the locals. We really like the **gothic style** of this restaurant, and we love their signature item, **the pretzel** after which it is so famously named, complimented with **delicious stews and soups** synonymous with the region.

Once your hunger has been satisfied, it's time to **feed your soul** with the cultural experience of a lifetime!

Not far away is the **Johann Strauss Museum**, which details his life and music in visual and audio stations. The museum opens at 2:00 pm.

And finally, you cannot visit the "**city of the waltz**" and not at least try your hand, or feet rather, at the art form. So after a hotel dinner or snack, as you may not be hungry after your feast at lunch, head over to the **Hop on Waltz** dance school where couples need no reservations. Lessons are €50 per couple, held in both English and German.

Location Information:

Joma
Address: Hoher Markt 10
Phone Number: +43 1 532 10 32
Website: http://www.joma-wien.at

Spanish Riding School
Address: Michaelerplatz 1
Phone Number: +43 1533 9031
Website: www.srs.at

Brezl Gwolb
Address: Ledererhof 9
Phone Number: + 43 533 8811
Website: http://www.brezl.at

Johann Strauss Museum
Address: Müllnergasse 3
Phone Number: +43 1 310 310 6
Website: http://www.wienmuseum.at/en.html

Hop on Waltz
Address: Friedrich-Schmidt-Platz 4
Phone Number: +43 1 405 26 69
Website:
http://www.tanzschulerueff.at/Tourismus/HOW.php

• Day 4 •

No trip to Austria can be complete without visiting the other romantic city of **Salzburg!** The Viator offers the perfect **day trip from Vienna to Salzburg**. A qualified guide will meet you and you'll be transported by coach through some of the most gorgeous landscape and scenery along the way. The trip is about 3 hours by car. Once you arrive in Salzburg, you'll visit the home of **Mozart** himself, take a wonderful walking tour through **Salzburg's Old Town**, and visit the **Mirabell Palace** gardens. Makes for a great day!

Location Information:

Viator: Salzburg Day Trip from Vienna
Phone Number: +888-651-9785
Website:
http://www.viator.com/tours/Vienna/Salzburg-Day-Trip-from-Vienna/d454-3585SALZBURG

• Day 5 •

It's time for some more fun! After a nice breakfast at your hotel, take the U-Bahn to Praterstern station; and if you are early enough, you may want to stop into the Austrian version of **Madame Tussauds**, which is right next door to Vienna's premier amusement park.

Featuring over 250 attractions, **Prater Park** caters to every age and every pace. There are plenty of places to keep your thirst quenched and your stomach full, and kiosks for snacks to nibble on in-between. There is also a **lovely park** right next door to the amusements and rides, so if you'd like to take a moment under the trees or ride along the mini train to enjoy the scenery, we recommend heading over to the inviting meadows of the **"Green Prater."**

If lunching amongst shrieks of delight from thrill seekers doesn't whet your appetite, then we suggest experiencing the Viennese markets in **Naschmarkt** or **Brunnenmarkt**. You'll find stalls piled high with tasty fruit, pastries, cheeses and wines. So be sure to **bring your backpack** along so you can make the trip back to your hotel comfortably. There are many options for ready to eat meals so **buy something for dinner** and take it back to your room and end the day on a relaxing note.

Location Information:

Madame Tussauds Wien
Address: Reisenradplatz, Prater
Phone Number: +43 1 890 33 66
Website:
https://www.madametussauds.com/Wien/en

Prater
Address: Praterstern, Prate
Phone Number: +43 1 40 00 80 42
Website: http://www.prater.at

Naschmarkt
Address: Wienzeile
Website:
http://www.wienernaschmarkt.eu/index.html

Brunnenmarkt
Address: Brunnengasse 16

• Best Places For Travelers on a Budget •

Vienna does have a few spots for the budget conscious but you may have to compromise on the location and tolerate a bit of city traffic. **So just bring your earplugs** along and the late night buzz shouldn't be a problem!

Bargain Viennese Sleeps

Koplinghaus Wien-Zentral is close to metro stations and central to the nightlife in Vienna. This hotel is a clean and inexpensive option for those looking to be in the hub of the city's activities. The majority of attractions are no more than 20 minutes away by train, which is just a stone's throw from the entrance.

Koplinghaus Wien-Zentral
Address: Gumpendorfer Strasse 39
Phone Number: +43 720 883262
Website: http://www.kolping-wien-zentral.at

Hotel Austria is located off the main roads on a quaint side street. This little hotel is the epitome of value for money. The rooms are spacious and well serviced with all the amenities you expect from a brand name hotel.

Hotel Austria
Address: Fleischmarkt 20/Wolfengasse 3
Phone Number: +43 720 115730
Website: http://www.hotelaustria-wien.at/en

Pension Suzanne is within earshot of the State Opera House. You hear the bells of the cathedral tolling each night, and since it is centrally located to all of the major tourists sites, getting around from here is a breeze.

Pension Suzanne
Address: Walfischgasse 4
Phone Number: +43 1 513 25 07
Website: http://www.pension-suzanne.at/index.en.php

Bargain Viennese Eats

You don't need to spend a fortune going out to Michelin star restaurants every night in order to experience the **delicious culinary culture** of Vienna. The alleyways and side streets offer great food at **affordable prices** that won't blow your budget. Here are our top recommendations:

One of our favorite Viennese spots for budget travelers is **Der Wiener Deewan**. It's centrally located near the Danube channel and the Votive church, and easily accessible by tram or subway. Here they serve delicious buffet-style Pakistani food with a 'pay as you wish' concept. Stop in to enjoy a variety of stews, salads, breads, rice and desserts, then pay the amount you think they deserve!

Der Wiener Deewan
Address: Liechtensteinstrasse 10
Phone Number: +43 925 1185
Website: http://deewan.at

Buffet Colloseum is open all day from 7:30 in the morning. This canteen style eatery attracts students from the nearby university because of its bountiful helpings and generous prices. The sausage with fries is a favorite among the ever-starving young adults so don't scoff.

Buffet Colloseum
Address: Nußdorfer Strasse 4
Phone Number: +43 1 3175107
Website: www.buffet-colosseum.at

Maschu Maschu is the place for yummy Mediterranean cooking at reasonable prices. The "very delicious" daily menu offers patrons falafel, pita and lemonade.

Maschu Maschu
Address: Neubaugasse 20
Phone Number: +43 1 9904 4713
Website: www.maschu-maschu.at

• Best Places For Ultimate Luxury •

You can stay in one of the household name hotels where the rooms, the décor and the service are all relatively standard, or you can partake of some of the customized luxuries on offer in some of Vienna's best boutique hotels.

Luxury Viennese Sleeps

Hotel Koning von Ungarn has a gorgeous open-air atrium that greets you as you sit down to enjoy your welcome drink...but that's only the tip of the luxury iceberg that awaits at this antique of Vienna. With **St. Stephan's Cathedral** looming overhead, the hotel boasts that **Mozart** composed from one of the rooms above the restaurant.

Hotel Koning von Ungarn
Address: Schulerstraße 10

Phone Number: +43 1 515 84 0
Website: http://www.kvu.at/en

Hotel Topazz is a modern hotel with classic finishes that embody what Vienna is all about. Hotel Topazz has 32 amazing rooms and a penthouse suite that **oozes luxury**. The rooms offer all the amenities guests have come to expect from the **upper echelon** of Viennese accommodations. The location could not be more convenient, with a plethora of coffee shops and attractions within walking distance.

Hotel Topazz
Address: Lichtensteg 3
Phone Number: +43 1 532 22 40
Website: http://www.hoteltopazz.com

Urbanauts was traditionally a workspace but has since been turned into an ergonomically interesting accommodation for those who live **outside the box** and want to holiday in places that reflect that. Formally art studios and office space, the unique lodging features private entrances in some of the lofts and showerheads that mimic rain. We think you'd really like it here!

Urbanauts
Address: Favoritenstrasse 17
Phone Number: +43 1 208 39 04
Website: http://www.urbanauts.at/en

Luxury Viennese Eats

The problem with eating out in Vienna is not where to find exquisite dining but rather which to choose from among the reams of high-society culinary spots. Home-style dishes or gastronomic chefs-d'oeuvre are all on offer in and around the city.

Steirereck was awarded a double Michelin star, and you must book a table well in advance to dine here. **Chef Reitbauer** serves diners plates so well arranged that it's almost a shame to eat them — well, *almost*.

Steirereck im Stadtpark
Address: Am Heumarkt 2A
Phone Number: +43 1 713 3168
Website: https://www.steirereck.at/en

Glacis Beisl is the locally celebrated spot where bistro meets haute cuisine — it's so cute! The food is great, and you're sure to be enchanted by a courtyard bedecked with fairy-lit trees and cobblestone floors.

Galcis Beisl
Address: Zugang Breite Gasse 4
Phone Number: +43 1 526 5660
Website: www.glacisbeisl.at

Walter Bauer is another of the city's Michelin starred eateries. Located on a side street in old Vienna, we think the buoyant, culinary flair here is unparalleled. The menu might be a bit limited, but only because the dishes are of the **highest quality**. We recommend trying the **duck breast** served with polenta.

Walter Bauer
Address: Sonnenfelsgasse 17
Phone Number: +43 1 5129871

• Vienna Nightlife •

Nightlife in Vienna is varied and magical. Cocktails and glasses of wine will get you in the mood to **shake your tail feather** in one of the many **hotspots** around the city. Public transport makes finding your way back to your hotel rather easy, within reason, of course. But the city of Vienna encourages you to sample all the good things it serves up after dark.

Great Bars in Vienna

In the Art Nouveau style, Loosbar is named after an Austrian architect, Adolf Loos, and it's where patrons can enjoy their drinks outside at modern tables against the backdrop of an outlandish building that dazzles the mind—which only gets worse as drinks begin to flow.

Loosbar
Address: Kärntner Durchgang 10,
Phone Number: +43 1 5123283
Website: www.loosbar.at

There are literally angels on the ceiling of the 'Red Angel' bar, **Roter Engel**. One of the iconic places at the heart of Vienna, this bar has been the downfall of many an upstanding individual. The atmosphere is conducive to a great night out.

Roter Engel
Address: Rabensteig 5
Phone Number: +43 1 5354105
Website: http://www.roterengel.at

Great Clubs in Vienna

Clubschiff is definitely the place to be for a great night out on the town. The music is infections and the urban atmosphere pulses with encouragement to dance the whole night away!

Clubschiff
Address: Schwedenplatz
Phone Number: +43 1 8950137
Website: http://clubschiff.co.at

Latino beats and Cuban cigars are some of the things that you will find at **Club Habana,** only blocks away from the State Opera House. The cocktails are heavenly — and they could even get shy wallflowers to do the cha cha or mambo!

Club Habana
Address: Mahlerstraße 11
Phone Number: +43 1 5132075
Website: http://clubhabana.at

Great Live Music in Vienna

3 decades old, **Jazzland** is dedicated to bringing all styles of the genre to delighted audiences, both local and international. The club is the largest of its kind in Vienna and night after night the stage has featured international and local stars. No other location will feed the soul of a **jazz and blues** lover quite like Jazzland.

Jazzland
Address: Franz-Josefs-Kai 29
Phone Number: +43 1 533 25 75
Website: http://www.jazzland.at/e_index.htm

Great Theatre in Vienna

There are so many iconic theatres in Vienna that you'll likely run out of time before you run out of venues and performances to see. **Some combine interests** to blissful perfection, such as the **Vienna Boys Choir** and the **Lipizzaner's** of the Spanish Riding School. These are our **top two recommendations** for a great night at the theatre.

Towering like a palace over the baroque-styled courtyard, the **Burgtheater** (National Theatre) was built in 1874 and has been a world leader in progressing the dramatic arts. Show tickets can be booked online and we recommend **booking seats here at the same time you're booking your flight to Vienna**.

Burgtheater
Address: Universitätsring 2
Phone Number: +43 51444 4140
Website: http://www.burgtheater.at

Located near the Museumsquartier, the **Theater am Spittelberg** (Spittelberg Theatre) is the "common" man's alternative to the National Theatre. This open-air theater features folk songs, comedy and even cabaret for those looking for a light-hearted night out in a venue where jeans are acceptable.

Theater am Spittelberg
Address: Spittelberggasse 10
Phone Number: +43 1 526 13 85

Website: http://www.theateramspittelberg.at

• Conclusion •

Vienna is a city that delights
the senses with the rich musical heritage of Mozart, Strauss, and Haydn. With the familiar one-two-three cadence of the Viennese waltz emanating from cafés and dance halls, you're sure to be enchanted with just how well the city blends romance and culture.

With the perfect cup of coffee or an exotic taste of wine in an upmarket vinothèque, the perfect place to soothe your ears, stimulate your mind or intoxicate your taste buds is certainly Austria's crowning jewel of Vienna!

Warmest regards,

The Passport to European Travel Guides Team

Visit our Blog! Grab more of our signature guides for all your travel needs!

http://www.passporttoeuropeantravelguides.blogspot.com

★ **Join our mailing list** ★ to follow our Travel Guide Series. You'll be automatically entered for a chance to win a **$100 Visa Gift Card** in our monthly drawings! Be sure to respond to the confirmation e-mail to complete the subscription.

• About the Authors •

PASSPORT TO
European Travel
The Best Travel Guides to Europe!

Passport to European Travel Guides is an eclectic team of international jet setters who know exactly what travelers and tourists want in a cut-to-the-chase, comprehensive travel guide that suits a wide range of budgets.

Our growing collection of distinguished European travel guides is guaranteed to give first-hand insight to each locale, complete with day-to-day, guided itineraries you won't want to miss!

We want our brand to be your official Passport to European Travel — one you can always count on!

Bon Voyage!

The Passport to European Travel Guides Team
http://www.passporttoeuropeantravelguides.blogspot.com

Made in the USA
Middletown, DE
13 March 2019